Theodore Roosevelt

A biography of an American President

Table of Contents

Introduction

Thank you for taking the time to read this book on Theodore Roosevelt!

This book aims to serve as a biography of Teddy Roosevelt, and details the incredible life he lived, as well as the large impact he had on the United States of America.

Throughout the following chapters, you will learn about Roosevelt's childhood, his formative years, his time at war, his politics, his family life, and much more!

As you will soon discover, much can be learned from the life and legacy of Theodore Roosevelt. At the completion of this book, you will be left with a great understanding of Theodore Roosevelt's life, and feel a deep respect for the man and the impact he had. Hopefully this book can inspire you to live as Theodore Roosevelt did; with passion, drive, and a desire to make the world a better place.

Once again, thanks for choosing this book, I hope you enjoy it!

Chapter 1: Early Life

The 26th president of the United States of America, Theodore Roosevelt Jr., was born on October 27, 1858 at East 20th Street, New York City. It is interesting to note that his early life actually helped to forge the man as history would recall him to be.

His father was Theodore Roosevelt Sr. and his mother was Martha Stewart "Mittie" Bulloch. His father was a wealthy businessman and also a philanthropist. His mother on the other hand was socialite and was well known in high circles. She came from a slave owning family that hailed from Georgia.

Theodore Roosevelt's Ancestry

Young Teddy Roosevelt was actually the second child in the family. He had three other siblings. Teddy was of Dutch descent, since his paternal grandfather was Dutch. However, the admixture of his ancestry came from his mother's side of the family.

From his mother's side of the stock, Teddy had an interesting mix in his ancestry. His mother was of Scottish as well as Scottish-Irish descent. Of course, they were also English as well. But those were not his only roots. He was also partly French, Welsh, and German.

The Challenge of Asthma

Did Theodore Roosevelt have an easy childhood? Well, given his family's background, he seemed to be set in life for fortune and maybe fame. But that wasn't necessarily the case for the young future president of the United States.

He had a thorn in the flesh as it were. One of the biggest challenges during the early life of the young Teddy Roosevelt was debilitating asthma as well as general poor health.

Due to the lack of sophistication in the field of medicine at the time, you couldn't say that this condition was easily dealt with, even with his family's vast resources.

It was reported that he would suffer night time asthma attacks, which he would describe as like being smothered to death.

His condition frightened his parents. What made things worse was the fact that even the best doctors of the time didn't have a cure, which exacerbated the feeling of helplessness in the family.

In consequence of his overall poor health condition, people called him "Teedie" which referenced a rather sickly and frail little boy. At this time, no one would imagine this frail little boy to be one who would lead soldiers into war

But in the long run, his health issues were just a minor setback – a childhood hiccup of growth as it were. It was a test for the young Teddy Roosevelt. If he could conquer this condition, he would be placed on the path of greatness.

Sparks of Greatness

In spite of the asthma attacks at night and what everyone around him would describe as poor health, the young Teddy Roosevelt was remarkably energetic in his young age.

In fact, he was mischievously inquisitive. He had a passion for learning and knowledge which he carried with him the rest of his life.

Believe or not, he was interested in zoology even at an early age. He was age seven when he first attempted to do anything related to the subject. At that early age he saw the carcass of a seal in the market.

This of course intrigued him, and he pursued to obtain part of it. Well, he got the animal's head. With the help of his cousins they proceeded to form what they would dub as their family's museum of natural history. Try to guess which animal's head did they try their hand at taxidermy with?

The seal was the first of many stuffed animals that were on display in the Roosevelt Museum. They would catch and kill animals, then later stuff them and put them on display. Even though the young Teddy Roosevelt only knew the rudiments of the craft, with the help of his cousins he became quite good at it.

Roosevelt studied the animals he had caught and then he prepared them for display in their makeshift museum.

He eventually wrote his own paper on the subject of insects. He was nine years old when he began to record his observation of different insects. The paper where he wrote his observations was entitled The Natural History of Insects.

Teen Years and Overcoming Physical Frailties

As the young Teddy Roosevelt grew older, he found that he could eventually keep up with his father when it came to physical exertion. In fact, he went on a hiking trip to the Alps with the rest the family in 1869.

This was actually one of the many family trips abroad that they would make in his early years. They toured Egypt in 1872, and they also made a couple of tours to Europe, one in 1869 and another in 1870. These trips he reported helped to shape his cosmopolitan point of view.

You can say that gradually and with concerted effort, the young Theodore Roosevelt was overcoming his childhood disability. In fact, he recalled that physical exertion actually benefitted him in that it helped to reduce the symptoms of his asthma.

He even began an exercise regime. After coming home from one camping trip, he enlisted a boxing coach to teach him how to strengthen his body and learn how to defend himself. He later related the fact that he was man-handled by two older boys during his stay in camp.

You can say that in his young age he was forging an indomitable spirit. It was one that doesn't give in to defeat or surrender to opposing forces. These things formed the foundation of his character and would serve him well as the leader of a nation and as soldier in times of war.

His Father's Influence

Theodore Roosevelt's father was nothing less than a role model for him. In fact, he was such an influence on the young man that Teddy would describe him as the "best man I ever knew."

He remembered how his father taught him and his siblings morals that would later guide him in life. He recalled how his father never tolerated lies and deceit, cowardice, idleness, or cruelty.

He would tenderly recollect how his father exemplified key virtues that he would apply to himself and his future family. Things like unselfishness, tenderness, gentleness, courage, and strength were all traits demonstrated by the older Roosevelt that eventually got passed on to his son, the future President.

Teddy Roosevelt's Education

We mentioned earlier that the young Theodore Roosevelt was afflicted by asthma during his younger years. This health condition along with his frail constitution prevented him from attending regular school.

That is why when he was young, he was taught by private tutors that were hired by his family. In spite of his physical condition, he actually excelled in his studies.

H.W. Brands, a biographer, noted that even though the young Teddy Roosevelt was no less than an intellectual giant, he had some difficulty in some areas of his studies. Roosevelt had difficulty mathematics as well as in the classical languages such as Greek and Latin.

Nevertheless, his curiosity and his hunger for knowledge were undeniable. And his interests were wide ranging. In September 27, 1876 he entered Harvard College, which is now of course known as Harvard University.

During his time at college, his father unfortunately died suddenly on February 9, 1878, which left him devastated.

He did well in most of his subjects as he doubled his efforts after the unfortunate setback. While he was outstanding in the field of biology and the sciences, Teddy Roosevelt still struggled in the classical languages of Greek and Latin. At that young age he was already a published ornithologist and also an accomplished naturalist.

He inherited from his father what would have amounted to $3.2-million in today's money (a total of $125,000 in their day).

He graduated from A. B. magna cum laude from Harvard in 1880. He also graduated Phi Beta Kappa, the leading honor society in the United States. Since idleness was frowned upon in the family, Teddy Roosevelt didn't slack off.

He shifted his interest from the study of natural science to law. He later attended Columbia Law School. However, the subject perplexed him and he found it to be irrational. Much of his time as a law student was spent writing a book called The War of 1812. This and his other writings were to be part of his lasting legacy.

Chapter 2: Early Political Career

Theodore Roosevelt's desire to take part in public affairs and public service was of course influenced by his father. The older Roosevelt was a leader in New York when it came to cultural affairs.

Roosevelt Sr. was a courageous figure in the eyes of the public, but especially so in the eyes of his son. Even though his in-laws were Confederate, Roosevelt Sr. was an avid supporter of the Union. This was eventually the path that Teddy Roosevelt would follow later in his life.

Early Stints in Politics

Teddy Roosevelt's early stints in the world of politics occurred while he was still attending Columbia Law School. It should be noted here that his peers steered clear of the chaos of America's politics at the time.

However, Roosevelt had an unlike mind – he was rather determined to enter the foray of the political world. During that time, he attended the meetings of the 21st District Republican Association in New York at the famed Morton Hall, which was on 59th street.

Again, we can see his father's influence here – note that his father was republican and was a prominent member of that party.

After some time, he defeated an incumbent assemblyman from the same party despite being quite new to the organization. Right after this electoral victory, Theodore Roosevelt decided to drop out of law school.

From 1882 to 1884 Theodore Roosevelt served as a member of the New York State Assembly. During his time there, he took an active part in the crackdown of corporate corruption issues.

He gained a positive and a very high political profile as evidenced in a lot of publications in New York when he exposed the potential corruption in Albany. He brought a possible collusion effort between Judge Theodore Westbrook and other involved parties to the public's attention.

He was able to push for an investigation to proceed. Of course, he was aiming to get Judge Westbrook to get impeached. He did not succeed in getting the judge impeached since the committee rejected the notion, but Roosevelt threw the proverbial monkey wrench into their plans during the process.

His win for his second term in 1882 was by a large margin. Later on, then President James Garfield was assassinated, and the Republican Party's Stalwart Faction was almost dissolved. This gave Teddy Roosevelt the opportunity to win the Republican Party leadership.

He bolstered and eventually won the passage of the civil service reform bill. His ally, Governor Cleveland, was influential in the passage of the said reform bill.

He won his second reelection the following year but lost his bid for the seat of State Assembly Speaker in New York. Later in his final term in the assembly, he became Chairman of the Committee on Affairs of Cities. During this final term in the assembly he was able to write bill after bill after bill – more than any legislator in his day ever made.

The Key Person from New York

Although he did not run for any political position in the presidential election of 1884, Theodore Roosevelt was active in the political circles that actively contested the available seats in government.

There were a lot of presidential hopefuls during that election year, which meant a lot of work needed to be done in order to ensure that your candidate stood out from the pack. Theodore

Roosevelt supported a colorless reformer, Vermont's Senator George F. Edmunds.

This went against what the state GOP preferred. They vetted for Chester Arthur of New York City. Arthur on his part passed the Pendleton Civil Service Reform Act.

However, unknown to the public, Chester was suffering from Bright's disease at the time, which would have contested his nomination. However, Chester did not disclose the fact and accepted the nomination out of duty.

Roosevelt worked tirelessly and was able to influence the delegates from Manhattan. He worked through the night and bargained with other influencers of his day. He eventually succeeded in gaining control of the state convention.

Teddy Roosevelt spoke at the GOP National Convention in 1884. His speech convinced the delegates to nominate John R. Lynch, an African American, and also a supporter of Edmunds. It was unfortunate however that James Blaine gained the support of the Edmund's delegates and thus won the nomination.

He also had the opportunity to address a huge crowd of ten thousand, which was the biggest audience he had ever addressed at the time. Having fought and lost and having had a chance to participate in national politics, Roosevelt lost any desire to dabble in the politics of the state.

He spent the remainder of his time during this period in his newly acquired Chimney Butte Ranch, which was located along the Little Missouri River. He did not take part in the party's activities to support their nominee during the general elections.

However, in order to maintain his role in the GOP he published a press release in July 19 of that year to voice his support for James G. Blaine who won their party's nomination. Of course, that meant losing the support of a lot of the reformers. After realizing that, he then decided to pack up and move to North Dakota having his mind made up to retire from politics – or so he thought.

Retirement as a Rancher

Judging from his upbringing, Roosevelt was never going to stand still or ever idle when he retired to Dakota living as a rancher. There, he published books on the life in the frontier. It would appear that his taste and destiny for leadership and public service wasn't over.

He organized and led other ranchers in an effort to address certain issues that affected everybody, such as the issue of overgrazing. His work here led to the formation of the Little Missouri Stockmen's Association.

He also organized the Boone and Crockett Club. They coordinated the conservation efforts of the game animals in the area.

His stint as a rancher ended during the winter of 1886-1887. That winter was rather harsh, and it wiped out the entirety of his livestock. His ranch wasn't the only ranch that suffered tremendous losses at the time. Even his competitors lost their investments as well.

This hampered his finances to a certain degree, and it also convinced him to return east back to New York. His experience here helped to mold him to be a man for the masses – a lesson that he would never have learned had he remained the ineffectual intellectual that he was during his early political career.

Chapter 3: Return to Public Service

When Theodore Roosevelt came back to New York after losing his investments in his farm in Dakota, he discovered that his peers in New York were also finding themselves in desperate times. He went back in 1886 and as soon as he returned the leaders of the Republican Party approached him.

They needed a party man to run for the position of mayor of New York City, and Roosevelt accepted. Was it the call of duty? Was it his desire for public service? We don't really know why he accepted their invitation to re-enter politics, despite the fact that he had very little hope of winning in that election.

His opponents in that campaign season consisted of Abram Hewitt, a democrat, and Henry George from the United Labor Party. Henry George as it would appear scared off the constituents due to the radical policies he instituted. Roosevelt on the other hand was a long-lost cause that had just returned from the frontier, which was essentially nowhere from the standpoint of New Yorkers.

Jumping into the flame of politics, Theodore Roosevelt fought and lost. The people feared George's policies, and so Hewitt won that election. This was another loss for Roosevelt who was still reeling from his previous loss.

Of course, Teddy Roosevelt feared that his political career might be over. As was his habit when things didn't look good, he retreated into a world of self-reflection.

He turned his attention to his writing. During this time, he wrote and published The Winning of the West. This work chronicled the American westward track, and was a huge success.

It received very favorable reviews and was a huge best seller at the time. It vindicated Theodore Roosevelt's penchant for success – not to mention the fact that it helped to boost his partially ailing finances.

Serving in the Civil Service Commission

Teddy Roosevelt later served in the Civil Service Commission. How did he gain that appointment? He gave stump speeches that were in support of Benjamin Harrison. Harrison won the presidential nomination during the Republican National Convention of 1888. His speeches were noticed and became highly regarded, which paved the way for his appointment.

He served in the commission until 1895. He was unlike his predecessors during his tenure there in the Civil Service Commission. He actually demanded and fought hard so that civil service laws would be enforced. On top of that he fought for the spoilsmen.

He often opposed and clashed with John Wanamaker, the postmaster general at the time. Wanamaker frequently dished out patronage positions to the supporters of Harrison – positions of course that these men didn't really deserve. In effect, Roosevelt fought to have them removed along with several postal workers.

In the next elections, Harrison unfortunately lost the bid for the presidential election of 1892 and Grover Cleveland won the nomination. In a strange twist of fate, Cleveland reappointed Roosevelt into the Civil Service Commission. It happened that Roosevelt's actions in booting out people from their service in the postal service affected Harrison's bid for the nomination – which of course helped Cleveland's campaign.

Serving as NYC Police Commissioner

Republican William Lafayette Strong, one who was strongly reform-minded, won the election and became New York City's mayor in 1894. He approached Theodore Roosevelt and offered him a position on the city's board of police commissioners.

Teddy accepted the offer and later became the board's president. During his term as president, he made a lot of radical changes.

Some of the reforms that he implemented along with the rest of the board of commissioners included annual physical examinations, along with regular inspections of the men in uniform's firearms.

They also implemented the appointment of recruits to the police force that would be based on the candidate's mental and physical qualifications. That meant the ditching of the old way of doing it – which was mainly based on the man's political affiliation. This of course gave more people who were better qualified and in need of jobs the option to enter the police force.

He also established the practice of awarding Meritorious Service Medals. It was a way to acknowledge the bravery and performance of the men in the police force. There were other systematic and not necessarily bold changes that he made as well.

He ordered that every police station should have its own telephone line, which of course improved the communications. He also established municipal lodging houses. During his tenure as president of the board of police commissioners, he fought and closed down police hostelries, which were actually places for corrupt practices.

Theodore Roosevelt also made it a habit to walk early in the morning or late at night to inspect policemen's beats, just to make sure that there were officers on duty. It wasn't easy, but it helped keep the citizens secure and it also helped to improve the efficiency of police service.

His career as police commissioner ended after he was informed by his party mates that legislation was being passed to dissolve the police commission. Roosevelt couldn't do anything but nod to the decision – he preferred to ascend to the order and decision rather than break away from his political party.

But that didn't mean he wouldn't do something about it in the future. You see a few years later he would win the governorship

of New York and would institute the office of the Police
Commissioner that would replace the police commission.

Chapter 4: Rough Riders and the War on Cuba

If you could see Theodore Roosevelt leading the First U.S. Volunteer Cavalry, you wouldn't suspect that he was once a frail little boy struggling with asthma. The day he led his troops in an uphill charge in Cuba he no longer was that sickly boy he once was. Teddy Roosevelt was now a powerful man.

But how did he end up in Cuba?

The Navy's Assistant Secretary

William McKinley won the nomination won the republican nomination during the presidential election of 1896. McKinley defeated William Bryan in that year's general election.

Even though Roosevelt initially backed the nomination of Thomas Reed, he opposed Bryan's platform of free silver, which meant he had to support McKinley's campaign eventually. On top of that, Roosevelt suspected and actually believed that Bryan's followers were, as he termed it, dangerous fanatics.

For his part and contribution to McKinley's presidential bid, he gave campaign speeches in his favor. After McKinley won in the election of 1897, Roosevelt was appointed as the Assistant Secretary of the Navy.

He served as second in command to John D. Long. As history would have it, the incumbent naval secretary was in poor health and wasn't really physically fit for any form of naval army work. On top of that he was more concerned about formalities rather than actually doing any soldiering.

That meant that a lot of the decisions that were to be made in the office of the naval command were left to Theodore Roosevelt, who took an active part in reforming the navy during his term.

It was Alfred Thayer Mahan who had a huge influence on Teddy Roosevelt at this time. He called for the strengthening of the country's naval forces. That meant that Roosevelt spearheaded the construction of more naval battleships.

Other than beefing up the country's navy, which was definitely needed at the time, Roosevelt also pushed for improving national security as well. He stressed his views about the country's need to participate in the affairs of other countries. He expressed these views and national security concerns to none other than the president of the country himself.

Roosevelt strongly urged that Spain should be made to leave Cuba, and that the Cubans should be given the freedom and independence that they seemed to desperately need at the time.

He stressed several important points. First, that the Cubans would benefit from their own independence, this would be grounded on principles of the country's self-interest and that of humanity as well.

He also stated that doing so would be a step forward towards complete freedom from the dominion of European countries. It would also elevate the mindset of the people, since they will focus their attention on something more than mere material gain. And finally, he believed that this military exercise would test and thus improve the country's military forces.

In spite of his efforts, McKinley and the other leaders of the country were reluctant to start a war with Spain. Remember that Spain historically was feared due to the strength of their navy.

Fate on the other hand had a different path in mind for the country and for Roosevelt as well. It was on the ill-fated day of 15 February 1898 when the USS Maine suddenly exploded in Cuba's harbor of Havana. The USS Maine was an armored cruiser and was difficult to sink.

When she exploded, hundreds of the crew members died in the wreckage. Of course, the US blamed Spain for the incident. McKinley for his part opted for a diplomatic solution to the issue. But Theodore Roosevelt on the other hand had other plans.

Roosevelt as the active head of the navy sent orders to all naval vessels to prepare for an upcoming war and possible encounters with the Spanish fleet.

These orders did not have the permission of either the President, or Long, Roosevelt's direct superior. In consequence of these orders, on May 1, 1898, Commodore George Dewey led the Asiatic Squadron and engaged the Spanish fleet in the Battle of Manila Bay. He later credited this victory to Roosevelt's orders.

This was the final spark needed to have the country fully engage Spain. Thus, McKinley asked Congress to declare war, after giving up on settling the matter via peaceful and diplomatic solutions.

And thus, began the Spanish-American War.

The Rough Riders Ride to Cuba

Theodore Roosevelt resigned from his position as the Assistant Naval Secretary in late April 1898 at the onset of the Spanish-American War. Colonel Leonard Wood and Roosevelt then formed what would be dubbed as the Rough Riders, or formally the First US Volunteer Cavalry Regiment.

It should be noted that Colonel Roosevelt's Rough Riders were only a temporary military formation. It was only to last until the end of the war with Spain.

When news of the formation of their regiment was announced in the papers, Roosevelt and Wood received hundreds of applications from all over the country. Roosevelt drew from his experience in the New York National Guard when they trained their troops in San Antonio, Texas.

It should be understandable why Teddy's family begged him to remain in office. However, Roosevelt was determined to see action. He was an outdoorsman and a patriot.

The Rough Riders were a mix of people from different walks of life. Their ranks included athletes, sheriffs, Native American tribesmen, men of the frontier, upscale gentlemen, Ivy Leaguers, and even cowboys.

Their regiment landed in Cuba on June 23, 1898. They used the speed and agility of their horses to gain positional and strategic advantage over their enemies. The Rough Riders fought against Spanish troops in the Battle of Las Guasimas, where the Spanish were eventually forced to abandon their positions.

Wood was then appointed to take command of the brigade and Roosevelt was promoted to Colonel and took charge of the entire Rough Rider regiment. This led to the crowning moment in Theodore's career in the military – the Battle of Kettle Hill.

Chapter 5: The Charge at Kettle Hill

The Rough Riders charge at Kettle Hill is the most popular military exploit in Theodore Roosevelt's career as a soldier. It is actually part of a larger military advance during the Spanish-American War, which is known as the Battle for the San Juan Heights.

There were two hills involved in this battle – the first one was San Juan Hill and the other one was Kettle Hill, as the soldiers who fought in the war called it. Both of these hills comprised the San Juan Heights, which was a strategic stand point for the siege of the nearby city of Santiago de Cuba.

In Theodore Roosevelt's mind, this battle was his defining moment. He called this moment his "crowded hour" and referred to it as a "great day of my life." This was actually a decisive battle in the entire war.

Cuba was one of the strongholds of Spain, and it was an economic center as well. From this place, tons of tobacco were exported to many countries throughout the world, including territories in the United States. Capturing Santiago de Cuba meant a great victory for the US, and it would be a crippling blow to Spain.

This was both the most famous battle in the Spanish-American War and also the bloodiest. This was also the greatest victory ever won by Theodore Roosevelt and his Rough Riders.

Attack on San Juan Heights

Hundreds of American Soldiers fell during the attack on San Juan Heights. Reports say that the cost of this battle was great as 200 men died during the charge of Kettle Hill, with more than 1,000 wounded. However, it should be noted that hundreds of regulars and soldiers from other regiments died even before reaching the base of San Juan Heights.

By July 3rd, the naval blockade that was maintained by Admiral William Sampson had already destroyed the Spanish fleet that was docked at the bay. After the siege of Santiago de Cuba, the Spanish surrendered the city on July 17.

The Charge on Kettle Hill

The role of the Rough Riders in this charge was to support the 10th Cavalry (i.e. the regulars, also known as the Buffalo Soldiers). Theodore Roosevelt's volunteer cavalry charged along with the 3rd Cavalry Regiment on the right flank of the Spanish position.

Lt. John H. Parker's Gatling Gun Detachment provided the cover fire, which opened a way for the troops to attack. The cavalry couldn't bring their horses to the top of the hills due to their steep incline and elevation of 2-kilometers.

All of the men except Theodore Roosevelt were on foot during that charge. He rode from one rifle pit to the next, up and down Kettle Hill to urge the advancement of the troops. When they first heard the Gatling guns fire they thought that they were Spanish machine guns aimed at them.

It made them pause momentarily, but they quickly recognized the familiar drumming.

You could hear the men shout as they rallied forward. Roosevelt described the battle as a time when he asked his men to do what other military writers deemed impossible. The Spanish defensive formation was tough and strategic.

Theodore Roosevelt commented that Parker's Gatling gun detachment deserved a lot more credit in the battle than he actually deserved himself. The heavy cover-fire the provided by those guns, which was an ingenious move actually, destroyed the morale of the enemy troops defending their positions.

The relentless hail of bullets made the Spanish defenders abandon their posts and retreat. This allowed the Rough Riders and the other American troops a chance to charge without fear of Spanish gun fire.

Of course, when they got to the summit of the hill there was some hand to hand combat involved. The Spanish soldiers didn't give up their defense completely. It should be noted that when the battle moved to the summit and the Spanish counter attack had to be fought off before they could secure Kettle Hill, that it was not just the Rough Riders who occupied the strategic territory.

American soldiers from different racial backgrounds fought side by side on that hill for the same cause. There were white men, men of color, and even Native Americans who fought and bled there. It was a show of force, and it was a united front.

Aftermath

Analysts and experts noted the huge casualties and losses that the American troops suffered. This moved the US Army to upgrade their weapons to the latest technology.

Sure, the Gatling guns were effective, but the fact shouldn't be left out of the books that the Spanish had the upper hand at one point due to their superior rifles and canons. As for the would-be president of the United States, this battle earned him the moniker "the colonel."

However, this name wouldn't stick that long since he would later be known by a more cherished and beloved nick name – "Teddy."

Within his inner circles, those who knew him best and those with whom he fought, his brothers in arms, they would fondly call him "The Colonel". Though to the rest of the country, he would be known as "Teddy."

Chapter 6: The Square Deal

By August 1898, Theodore Roosevelt and his men left Cuba to return to the United States. Upon arrival, they were quarantined for a short time due to fear of spreading yellow fever.

It wasn't long after his return from the war that Lemuel E. Quigg, a Republican Congressman, came to visit. It didn't take long for their party to call upon Roosevelt again to rally their cause.

The incumbent party boss, Tom Platt, never really liked Theodore Roosevelt due to his characteristic independence and unwillingness to buckle down and nod to Republican Party bosses.

However, Platt had no choice since their next best option wasn't exactly a popular choice – the incumbent governor Frank S. Black.

The Gubernatorial Election of 1898

Theodore Roosevelt agreed to become the nominee of the Republican Party for this election. And on top of that he also agreed not to "make war" with the party bosses after he was elected.

Roosevelt won that election and became the governor of New York. As they feared Roosevelt winning the gubernatorial race was a double-edged sword – yes, he went against the wishes of the party bosses.

As governor, he faced large scale problems like conservation, labor relations, monopolies, and trusts. During his term, Roosevelt introduced a platform that was based on what he called The Square Deal.

The principles behind the Square Deal included the following:

- The subordination of the local and party concerns to the concerns of the state
- Equitable sharing of responsibilities and privileges
- Honesty in public affairs

One innovation that he introduced during this time was holding two press conferences each day. This allowed him to be visible to the voting public and to reach out to the masses – well specifically to the middle class, which was his political base no less.

Party boss Platt and Roosevelt did not see eye to eye on many issues. At times, Roosevelt would reluctantly agree with his party's leadership but would later make his own decisions, even if it contradicted what the party bosses may have wanted.

For instance, he pushed for the Ford Franchise-Tax bill. This bill gave them the power to tax public franchises. Platt insisted that Roosevelt should consult him whenever an appointment had to be made to positions that affected major policy decisions.

He appeared to agree at first, but then he made up his own mind about who to appoint to what position. In effect, Roosevelt appointed many capable men and it appeared that they were with Platt's approval.

Politics was a careful dance where you tried to avoid stepping on everyone's toes while still reaching your desired spot on the dance floor. And we can say that Theodore Roosevelt danced well.

A lot of what he did at this time, as one historian carefully observed, helped to shape what Roosevelt would do when he became president. He mediated conflicts between the labor force and the capital owners. He regulated railroad rates.

He became more public, thus gaining the trust of the general public. He was at the forefront of conservation efforts. And one final thing — he was at the forefront when it came to the protection of the less fortunate.

After seeing his performance as governor, a lot of people suggested that he should run for president. After all, he was doing great as he led the most populous state in the entire union.

However, if he did run for the presidential seat he would be going against McKinley, which was something that he would never want to do considering their long and tested relationship.

Chapter 7: Vice President

One of the reasons why Theodore Roosevelt did not want to run for the office of Vice President is the fact that it was nothing more than a powerless office. On top of that, McKinley had already informed Roosevelt that he did not want to nominate Roosevelt for the vice presidential seat due to his actions prior to the Spanish-American War.

Thomas Platt, the party boss of the Republicans, wanted to be rid of Theodore Roosevelt. The two did not agree on a lot of matters and making Roosevelt run for vice president would mean that he would vacate the governor's seat.

To execute such a plan, Platt used a series of newspaper campaigns that were in favor of Roosevelt. They promoted his nomination to the vice presidency. The two met in the Republican National Convention in 1900.

In that discussion, Roosevelt agreed that he would accept the vice-presidential nomination, that is if the convention should offer it to him. If not, then he would seek another term as governor of New York City.

Platt sort of underhanded Teddy in that he went to Matthew Quay, the party boss of the republicans in Pennsylvania. He asked Quay to campaign for the nomination of Theodore Roosevelt, which he did. As a result, Roosevelt was handed the nomination for the vice-presidential ticket – and that basically solved Platt's problems with Roosevelt for the time being. Roosevelt actually won the nomination unanimously.

Theodore Roosevelt's opponent in the upcoming elections was William Jennings Bryan from the Democratic Party. You can say that Bryan was equally energetic in his campaign as Roosevelt was.

Both men supported the war with Spain and that area was a no contest. The huge bulk of the controversy and contest between the two was the annexation of the Philippines as part of the aftermath of the war.

For William Jennings Bryan, doing so was the equivalent to imperialism – the very reason (well, one of the reasons) why they went to war with Spain. He argued that the annexation of the Philippine islands would spoil whatever innocence America had claimed.

In his mind, doing so would mean that they were committing the very same practice that they fought against.

Theodore Roosevelt on the other hand thought otherwise and disagreed with Bryan's views. He said that it would be best for the Philippines to have the stability that the United States offered.

It was a time of peace, and in the minds of the voting public, what America did for the Filipinos was something to be proud of. The country sent school teachers and provided them with resources that could help them start anew as a people.

At the conclusion of this debate, it was clear that the people sided with Roosevelt's views. Roosevelt was sworn into office in March 1901. It was a victory – but it was not the type of victory that he preferred.

You see, the office of the vice president then was one without power. He had practically no influence while serving as vice president. This did not suit his rather active temperament. He was a man of action, and in this office there was nothing to act upon.

This gave him time to vacation and relax though, so he traveled. There were a few duties that he had to dispense with like presiding over the senate. But that only took 4 days and then the senate adjourned. After that he was left with practically nothing to do.

On one occasion, on September 2, 1901 he published his famous aphorism "Speak softly and carry a big stick, and you will go far."

We can say that this was a moment of recoil for Theodore Roosevelt, the man of action. It can also be viewed as a short break from work – something that he and his family needed at the time.

Roosevelt was vacationing in Vermont when he received news that President McKinley was shot and was in the hospital. However, the President seemed to be in a stable condition and was reported to be recovering well – so off he went and resumed his vacation.

Soon after however, he would be informed that the US president's condition was worsening and later he would learn that the man had died. Thus, his vacation, R&R, and term of service as Vice President were cut short.

Chapter 8: Roosevelt the President

The Unexpected Path to the US Presidency

Then US President McKinley was shot by a deranged anarchist on September 6, 1901. McKinley was visiting Buffalo, New York for the Pan-American Exposition at the time. He appeared to be making a steady recovery, and it seemed that he would soon be back on his feet.

However, tragedy befell them when McKinley's condition worsened, and he died eight days later. At the time, Roosevelt was on his way back to Buffalo after having been informed of the president's then worsening condition.

He didn't make it to see McKinley alive. He was informed of the president's passing while he was in North Creek. Theodore Roosevelt continued on his travels and arrived in Buffalo. When he arrived there, Ansley Wilcox House swore him in as the nation's 26th president– he was then the youngest president in the country's history at the age of 42.

The New US President

His youth and vigor changed the public image of the office of the President. Teddy Roosevelt as was his custom would eventually shake things up and make radical changes that reshaped the entire nation as a whole.

However, since Roosevelt was now sworn in as the next president of the nation, the office of the vice president was left vacant. There was no provision in the country's laws about any intra-term vacancies that may occur. This was something that would be amended in 1967 in the 25th Amendment. That meant that Theodore Roosevelt had no standing vice president when he served his first term.

During his first term of service he assured McKinley's supporters that he would adhere to the policies that were established by his predecessor. That was good news for those who supported the former US president.

However, Roosevelt's succession to the US Presidency was ill news to his detractors.

Mark Hanna was particularly bitter when he received the news. Remember that he opposed Roosevelt's nomination to the vice presidency during the national convention.

Once Roosevelt had taken the highest electoral position in the country, he almost immediately sought to become the Republican Party's leader. Always the forward thinker, Teddy took great efforts to bolster his position as the nation's leader and to secure his place in the coming elections in 1904.

Domestic Policies

As president of the United States of America we can glean from past experience as to what Theodore Roosevelt would be doing in that office – busting corruption and making radical changes to reshape the current infrastructure.

That was basically the effect of his political agenda, which was again influenced heavily by his upbringing under the tutelage of his father, of course. He would regulate trusts, and took measures to restrain those who charged unfair prices. For instance, he would use the Sherman Antitrust Act of 1890 rather aggressively.

He also proposed the creation of the United States Department of Commerce and Labor, as well as the Bureau of Corporations. These would act as regulating bodies for big businesses, which Roosevelt saw as an integral part of the country's economy.

As usual, he was also a man of the people. He helped to settle a labor dispute between coal miners and J.P. Morgan. Again, he made popular his policy of a Square Deal. The miners received higher wages in effect.

It couldn't be denied that Teddy Roosevelt was a true conservationist deep within. Considered as the very first major legislative success of his administration, they enacted the National Reclamation Act of 1902.

It provided support to irrigation projects on a large scale in the West. His administration was also responsible for dedicating almost 200 acres of wildlife refuges, reserves, and national forests. This was roughly five times more than what all of his predecessors had ever done, combined.

Due to his clashes with big business in the effort to regulate trade, Teddy Roosevelt was often dubbed as the "trust buster." However, he was still able to gain the trust and support of conservative republicans. Thus, he was also the first to win a reelection after gaining the office of the presidency due to the death of the previous US president.

Foreign Policy

Just as Roosevelt had promised McKinley's supporters, his foreign policy fell in line with that of his predecessor. Like McKinley, Teddy Roosevelt sought to move the entire nation and take responsibility as one of the world's most powerful nations. The country was to be in effect a big brother to smaller nations. During his term, America was now shedding its old practice of isolationism.

He believed that the President of the United States should be more than willing to backup any diplomatic negotiations with a show of force – and use force if need be. This was of course within the realms of Roosevelt's "speak softly and carry a big stick" policy.

For instance, in 1903 he used this policy to help Colombia, which made Panama secede. This of course helped to initiate and speed up the construction of the Panama Canal. The countries in Latin America were not the only recipients of Roosevelt's big stick.

In fact, these countries benefited from it too; especially when it was other countries that were on the wrong end of that proverbial stick. For example, during Theodore Roosevelt's administration, several European countries wanted to collect on debts that were owed to them by Latin American countries, albeit by force.

The US under Roosevelt interceded and issued what would be a corollary to the Monroe Doctrine. We can recall what then President James Monroe asserted in December of 1823, stating:

"The American continents ... are henceforth not to be considered as subjects for future colonization by any European powers."

Teddy Roosevelt's version of course was slightly different. He stated that the US would bar any form of foreign intervention. The country would ensure that Latin American countries paid their debt. Thus, no bullying from European countries was executed, and the countries in debt were able to make their payments as needed.

During his last year as President of the United States, Theodore Roosevelt beefed up the strength of the US Navy. It would become a major force to reckon with compared to other armies in the world.

Roosevelt headed the negotiations, with his "big stick" at hand of course, during the Russo-Japanese War in 1904.

Chapter 9: Life After the White House

Now, even though we can say for a fact that Theodore Roosevelt was still vigorous and young when he ended his second term as President of the United States, he acquiesced and never ran for another term.

This was part of a promise he made earlier, which of course he was bound to fulfill. He himself admitted that this limitation of presidential terms was a safety net of sorts that protected the country from dictatorship and tyranny.

Nevertheless, when the elections of 1908 came along, he grudgingly fulfilled the pledge he made during the campaign period back in 1904. He bowed out of the electoral race and threw his support in favor of William Howard Taft.

African Safari

After leaving the White House, Roosevelt went on a safari that was sponsored in large part by Andrew Carnegie. The safari was dubbed the Smithsonian-Roosevelt African Expedition.

Their hunting party included scientists from the Smithsonian Institute. A lot of other colorful and well-known outdoorsmen joined them, which included John Alden Loring, Edgar Alexander Mearns, Kermit Roosevelt, and Edmund Heller. Their party leader was none other than the legendary big game hunter RJ Cunninghame.

The expedition lasted for 10 months and they traveled to many different parts of Africa. They hunted in parts of Kenya as we know it now, but back then it was known as Mombasa. From there they traveled to the Congo, Sudan, and Egypt.

They trapped and killed 11,400 animals during this expedition all in the name of science. The specimens were shipped back to the Smithsonian with the Museum of Natural History along with other museums benefiting from the spoils of the expedition.

He then toured Europe and met with foreign leaders which included Kaiser Wilhelm II of Germany, Emperor Franz Joseph of Austria-Hungary, and King George V of Great Britain.

He also gave a speech in Oslo Norway where he urged his listeners to hasten the amendments necessary to strengthen the Permanent Court of Arbitration. He eventually traveled back to the United States in June of 1910.

The Republicans Divided

Much to his dismay, then President William Howard Taft failed to follow through with his promise of enforcing progressive reforms. He fell back to a set of rather conservative reforms instead. This of course enraged Roosevelt who then campaigned in 1912 against Taft's nomination, which eventually failed.

This divided the republicans, with those supporting Roosevelt leaving to form what would be known as the Progressive Party. They were also dubbed as the Bull Moose Party, in reference to Roosevelt once referring to himself as being as strong as a bull moose.

The effect of this schism in the Republican Party was a loss in the general elections, and the Democrats won the White House with Widrow Wilson as President of the United States, taking 435 electoral votes to Taft's dismal 8 electoral votes during the elections.

Roosevelt for the most part was a success in this electoral run. He was able to amass 88 electoral votes, which is still the most successful third party bid in any elections of the United States.

Chapter 10: Family Life

His Love for His Children

To the world he was the President, he was the colonel, he was the Dakota hunter, the frontiersman, a Nobel Prize winner, and many other things. However, it was no secret that perhaps his greatest legacy that he ever left on earth was his children.

Theodore Roosevelt was away from home many times, especially during the active years of his career in politics. He traveled far and wide on rail and other means of transport to campaign.

Sometimes, he campaigned for his own stake at the polls and at other times he did it for other politicians and Republican party mates. He wrote and published press releases and attended press conferences. He attended GOP and other political meetings.

Other times, he went on safaris to many different countries. Occasionally he brought the entire family along, but there were plenty of times when he traveled by himself, or just with other enthusiasts of the outdoors.

And there were times when he would leave to go to war.

Such was the duty of Theodore Roosevelt. However, it cannot be denied that when he was far from home, especially when his children were still young that they would be at the forefront in his mind.

He held them dearly in his heart. The evidence was a trail of letters which he wrote them while he was away. In them you will find the deepest expressions of love and care of a parent for his offspring. The letters were often illustrated, and they also contained his reflections while he was away.

The said letters were compiled and were subsequently published in book form. The book or letter collection was published in 1919 as "Theodore Roosevelt's Letters to his Children" and it became a best seller.

Marriages

Theodore Roosevelt was first married to Alice Hathaway Lee, with whom he had one daughter, Alice Lee Roosevelt. Their daughter was born on February 12, 1884 and unfortunately the mother died two days after giving birth. She died due to kidney failure.

It was a tragic time for Teddy Roosevelt. In that same year his mother "Mittie" also died. He wrote in his journal saying in effect that a light had gone out in his life.

Roosevelt was married a second time to his childhood friend Edith Kermit Carow on December 2, 1886. With her he had five children: Theodore III, Kermit, Ethel, Archibald, and Quentin. The happy couple had an enduring and happy relationship that lasted 30 years, up until the day Teddy Roosevelt died.

Chapter 11: Winning the Nobel Prize

Theodore Roosevelt was the first statesman to ever be awarded the Nobel Peace Prize. At the time of its awarding it was quite controversial, and some said that the great Alfred Nobel would have been turning in his grave when the announcement was made.

He was given the Nobel Prize for negotiating for peace during the Russo-Japanese War which lasted from 1904 to 1905. Other than that, he also negotiated and resolved disputes in Mexico via arbitration, which was actually a recommendation made by the peace movement.

Critics had a lot to say and protest about this award. For instance, it was said that Norway awarded Roosevelt the Nobel Prize as a favor in order to win friends who held power in other countries. It should be noted that at the time the Nobel Prize was awarded to Roosevelt, Norway had parted ways in the union with Sweden.

Some said that Teddy Roosevelt wasn't deserving of the award since he was an imperialist. They said that he was responsible for America's conquest of the Philippine islands.

Of course, Theodore Roosevelt had his detractors in his day. You just can't please everybody. However, if you looked at his policies and the way he conducted his presidency, you will see that he was a radical whilst serving under the Republican Party.

He detested the conservative wing of his political party and pushed for a lot of changes. As you can see from the details that we have presented here in this book, he was a strong proponent of social reforms.

He moved for state control of the nation's capital. He often went out of his way to settle disputes and protect laborers. His arbitration and efforts for peace were evidenced in the United States, as well as abroad in other countries.

He was a soldier, and yes he participated in real combat. He knew how difficult it was in the field of battle because he led his men there. At the outbreak of World War I he tried to enlist as an army officer but was denied the opportunity to serve.

Chapter 12: Interesting Facts About Theodore Roosevelt

Much can be said about Theodore Roosevelt, since he was a very colorful man and he was truly multifaceted. The following are some of the most interesting facts about Theodore Roosevelt:

1. The Teddy Bear

All throughout this book we have referred to him as "Teddy Roosevelt." He would have hated that if he were alive to read through these pages. He despised the moniker ever since the day the papers first published it.

He preferred to be called by his first name, Theodore. Those who were closest to him, which included his compatriots during the war, referred to him as The Colonel or simply Colonel.

So, what's the deal with Teddy and the Teddy Bear?

While President, Theodore Roosevelt was on a hunting trip in Mississippi. The guides had arranged to have an old bear tied to a tree so the president could shoot it. When Roosevelt arrived at the scene, he refused to shoot the bear – someone else had to shoot it.

This act of mercy on the sporting grounds was later translated into a newspaper cartoon. The cartoon then inspired a local toy maker to sell stuffed toy bears. He even asked permission from Roosevelt to make these stuffed bears. These bears came to be known as the "Teddy Bear."

2. The Martial Artist

Earlier in this book we mentioned that Teddy Roosevelt took boxing lessons after being bullied by older boys during a camping trip. He actually continued in this fighting art and was rather good at it.

He often sparred several times a week and he even continued sparring while he was President. One boxer he sparred with actually hit him too hard in the face, detaching his retina and blinding him in one eye. He ended his boxing training in 1908, and switched to jiu-jitsu instead.

3. A college dropout – well not exactly

We know that Roosevelt graduated from Harvard. However, he undertook graduate studies in the field of law at Columbia. However, he lost focus on his legal studies and dropped out of his graduate studies to begin his political career.

4. The father of the modern US Navy

Theodore Roosevelt authored a book on naval warfare that eventually became a standard textbook of study. His scholarship on the naval war of 1812 is still cited today. During his service in government, he sent the US Navy on a worldwide tour as a show of strength back in 1907.

5. The prolific writer

We have mentioned here in this book a number of times how Theodore Roosevelt would retreat from the cares of the world to write. He was actually a prolific writer. He wrote on a number of subjects. He wrote and published a total of 35 books, and he also wrote an estimated 150,000 letters.

6. An incredible memory

We also highlighted the fact early in this book how the young Roosevelt had an almost impeccable memory. He even claimed that he had a photographic memory, though we cannot establish this claim for a fact. However, one of his biographers, Edmund Morris testified that Roosevelt could quote vast amounts of content, including some obscure poetry well over a decade after last reading it.

7. First President to win a Nobel prize

As we have mentioned earlier, Theodore Roosevelt had a very aggressive foreign policy. Nevertheless, he moved the United States of America into a position of peacemaker in the global community.

We mentioned in a separate chapter that Roosevelt mediated between two warring countries in 1906 - Russia and Japan. He was able to push for peace between the two countries and because of that he was awarded the Nobel Peace Prize.

He was the first President to ever be honored with such an award. The world also saw him being the mediator again in another dispute between two nations –Germany and France. He settled their dispute over the division of Morocco.

8. He was a child taxidermist

Teddy Roosevelt was an inquisitive little boy when he was young. He was so passionate for learning about wildlife that he learned taxidermy before he reached his teenage years. He traveled around with his tools, which included arsenic among other things.

9. Wimp to warrior

Theodore Roosevelt was remarkably wimpy when he was a kid. He overcame this adversity and became an active weightlifter and boxer. He was a fitness advocate until the day he died at age 60.

10. Harvard's odd man out

Most of his Harvard peers were more conservative and subdued. Teddy stood out in the crowd for his rather boisterous nature. He would often yell at a friend from across the grass when he saw one. His friends described how he would emphasize a point by hammering his fist into his palm.

11. Just a jealous guy

His first wife, Alice Lee, attended Harvard as well and that was where their courtship began.

Their peers observed Theodore as man who would easily get jealous. In fact, he was said to be over-protective of his "turf."

He even challenged other men to a duel when a guy would have the guts to approach Alice and hint at the possibility of calling on her. Teddy even mail ordered a pair of French pistols just in case someone would take him up on the challenge.

12. The Dakota Cowboy

At one point in his life he retreated to Dakota; that was in 1883. There, he established his very own ranch and became a cowboy – complete with spurs and a buck skin shirt. He even helped to organize the ranchers in the area.

He loved the outdoors and he felt at home with guns on his hips, horses in the barn, and cattle all around him. All of that ended after an extreme winter that cost him his entire livestock.

13. The youngest president in history

To date, Theodore Roosevelt still remains the youngest man to become the president of the United States. He was just 42 years old when he was sworn into office. The next youngest President in the history of the nation was John F. Kennedy who was 43 when he became president. Third on the list was Bill Clinton at 46 years old.

14. He was eye candy for the press

Theodore Roosevelt was a man of flare, which the press and media loved. In fact, he used this particular charm of his to nudge the public's opinion in his favor. He dedicated a room in the White House and made it his press room.

He also had a flare for publicity stunts. For instance, he invited press people for candid and informal talks while he was shaving. He himself field tested a submarine, and there was one time when he rode on horseback for 98 miles. He loved the media attention these stunts attracted.

15. He cleaned up the meat processing industry in the USA

In 1906 President Roosevelt passed into law two important pieces of legislature that changed and improved meat processing and food handling processes in the country: the Meat Inspection Act and the Pure Food and Drug Act.

16. He saved football

Do you know that we would not have professional football today if not for Roosevelt? Before the NFL entered the limelight, the game of football itself was almost removed as a sport. From 1900 to 1905, 45 football players died from game related injuries.

Injuries included broken backs and broken necks. The general public wanted to have the games stopped. Teddy Roosevelt called upon various experts from different schools like Harvard and Yale, and they discussed ways to improve the safety of the players.

And that was how safety equipment and modern game rules as we know them today were developed. Its notorious mortality rate dropped, and the game thrived.

17. He had his own private zoo in the White House

During his term as President you shouldn't have been surprised to find an assortment of different animals in the White House. Of course, you'd see the usual dogs as well as cats. But there were also snakes, bears, chickens, flying squirrels, a zebra, and a lion.

18. He burned his own Presidential portrait

He didn't like the Presidential portrait that was made for him. He said that it made him look like a "mewing cat." His children even teased him about it. He actually hated it, but it got displayed anyway – it was even on display in France. Roosevelt burned the darn thing when it was finally returned to the White House. That was one of the last things that he did as President of the United States.

17. First US president to travel abroad while in office

No US president before him left the country while serving their term. Maybe it was a security concern, but we can't know for sure. He visited Panama in 1906 to see how the construction on the Panama Canal was moving along. He even operated one of the steam shovels while he was there.

18. He went skinny dipping while the French ambassador was visiting

Gifford Pinchot, his Division of Forestry chief was with him naked in the water at the time. The French ambassador opted to kept his clothes on for fear that some ladies may come along.

19. Theodore Roosevelt had a chest tattoo

Teddy Roosevelt wasn't the first president of the United States to sport a tattoo, though it wasn't a common thing at the time.

Another US president, Andrew Jackson, had a tomahawk tat inked on his thigh. Teddy Roosevelt on the other hand had his tattoo on his chest – the Roosevelt family crest.

20. He was a big coffee drinker

The Roosevelt kids often described their father drinking coffee from a mug the size of a tub. He even sweetened his coffee with seven lumps of sugar.

21. A speed reader

Theodore Roosevelt was known to consistently read one book a day.

22. He still gave a speech after he was shot

After the assassination attempt on him on 14th of October 1912, he still gave his speech even though he had a bullet in his chest. Of course, they rushed him to the hospital to remove the bullet right after.

23. Theodore and Houdini

The Library of Congress has a picture of Roosevelt standing side by side with Harry Houdini.

Chapter 13: Death

Theodore Roosevelt died on the night of January 6, 1919 in his estate on Sagamore Hill, which was overlooking Long Island.

The night before, January 5th, he received treatment from Dr. George W. Faller since he reportedly had breathing problems. Feeling much better after the treatment he retired to bed.

Last Words

James Amos, their family servant, reported that the last thing that the good Theodore Roosevelt said to him was "Please put out that light, James" – little did he know that these were the very last words that the man would utter in his lifetime.

Cause of Death

It was reported that Theodore Roosevelt died in his sleep somewhere between 4 AM and 4:15 AM. Medical reports state that a blood clot detached from one of his veins which subsequently entered into his lungs. He was 60 years old when he died.

Cheating Death

Theodore Roosevelt cheated death many times in his life. He was an adventurer, and wasn't afraid to put himself in danger.

He was as much the people's hero as anyone can imagine. You can say that his solution to many of the ills that plagued the world was to roll up his sleeves and punch the problems into submission. But as we all know, sometimes life punches back.

For instance, there was a time when he was accosted by thieves and he was left stranded, almost freezing to death.

He served as deputy sheriff in North Dakota in 1886. Three thieves cut the mooring line of his boat. The boat drifted down the Little Missouri River which was at freezing temperatures. The rapids were already ice choked. Surprisingly, Roosevelt was able to get ashore and made it home alive and well.

In fact, Roosevelt and his companions managed to capture the thieves after three days of struggle in the icy river. They fought the rapids in a makeshift boat and paddle.

Three times in the Spanish-American war Teddy Roosevelt escaped the clutches of death. Several times he was almost killed in combat. Upon landing in Cuba, their commanding officer ordered the Rough Riders to attack the fortified Spanish positions.

Of course, they came under fire, but the maneuver worked and the defending Spanish soldiers retreated. 7 of their men died and 7 others were wounded. Theodore Roosevelt on the other hand was unscathed in spite of heavy gunfire.

Another incident occurred during their assault on Kettle Hill. Colonel Roosevelt was on horseback and signaled the charge. However, his men, the Rough Riders, didn't hear him, and thus he was left charging by himself.

He came under enemy fire and only then did he realize that there was no one but a handful of his men behind him. He had to turn around and come back to the rest of his troops and give the order to charge once again.

However, this time his horse got entangled in barbwire, so he had to lead the charge on foot. He was the first to get into enemy positions and he managed to kill a Spanish soldier which allowed his men to continue the charge up Kettle Hill.

Death didn't just come for good old Teddy Roosevelt during times of war. It even came for the good President during times of relative peace. One such time was in 1902, whilst Roosevelt was with a party on a carriage.

They were struck by an electric street car that was speeding. The impact sent him hurling and he landed on the ground with a minor facial injury. His leg was severely injured, and he required surgery. He had rely on a wheelchair for some time during his recovery.

Perhaps his closest brush with death occurred when he was shot point blank in the chest. He was no stranger to gun fights, but he was certainly not expecting to be involved in one at the time.

He was running for a term and the day of the elections was three weeks away. A lone gunman fired at Roosevelt. The assassin got close enough to fire a single round at point blank into his chest.

Fortunately, he had a 50-page copy of the speech that he was supposed to give that day in his chest pocket, and it was located behind his steel case for his glasses. That was enough to dampen the impact and save his life.

Burial Ceremonies

Thomas Marshall was quoted for having said that *"Death had to take Roosevelt sleeping, for if he had been awake, there would have been a fight."* Marshall was Roosevelt's vice president during his term.

Among his children, it was Archibald who first learned of their father's passing. He telegraphed his brothers and sisters informing them of their father's demise.

The family held a private service at Sagamore Hill's North Room. It was later followed by a modest funeral service at Christ Episcopal Church. In attendance were some of the Roosevelt's dearest comrades, which included William Howard Taft, Henry Cabot Lodge, Warren Harding, Charles Evans Hughes, and Thomas R. Marshall.

Theodore Roosevelt was then buried on a hillside at Youngs Memorial Cemetery. Spectators lined the procession despite the heavy snow. A squad of New York City policemen rode all the way there as an escort. The burial site had a lovely overlooking view of Oyster Bay.

Chapter 14: His Legacy

It cannot be disputed that Theodore Roosevelt was the first modern president of the United States. The influence and the stature of the office of the President in today's modern government began with his efforts to put the presidency at the forefront of public service.

Before he was sworn to office for the very first time, previous Presidents didn't express the same level of authority he had in his day. It was Congress and the political parties that moved the nation and the government's policy making machinery.

Through aggressive executive action, he made full use of the all the powers of the executive office and established its strong relationship with the people. He challenged the notion of a limited government which was prevalent at the time. He insisted and made it his policy that the government should be the cause of social and political reforms on behalf, and for the people, of the United States.

During his term, the White House became the focal point when it came to welfare legislation. He spearheaded the conservation movement, which is why we have plenty of wildlife reserves and national parks where everyone can enjoy Mother Nature and all her creatures.

President Roosevelt also changed government's dealings with big business. He setup regulatory bodies to ensure that corporations did not have carte blanche powers. He wanted to make the market equitable and fair to all people.

However, he did not challenge the status of corporations and other big businesses in America. Being an economist, he believed that these large companies were integral to the growth of the nation's economy.

Theodore Roosevelt was also the one to place the United States at the forefront on the world stage. He changed the country's status from that of an isolationist to that of a mediator and a worldwide super power.

Come to think of it, all of this began during his formative years learning about the principles of justice, equality, and a love of all mankind from his father who was his exemplar.

Conclusion

Thanks again for taking the time to read this book!

You should now have a good understanding of Theodore Roosevelt's life, and the incredible impact he had!

If you enjoyed this book, please take the time to leave me a review on Amazon. I appreciate your honest feedback, and it really helps me to continue producing high quality books.